C000154360

ROBERT BURNS - NATURE

TWELVE WORKS INSPIRED BY NATURE

ALASTAIR TURNBULL

Contents

Big **R**ed **R**esources

A Brief Introduction to Robert Burns

Robert Burns was born on the 25th of January 1759 in a small cottage in Ayrshire, the first of six sons and daughters to William and Agnes Burnes. He was born into what we would now call "abject poverty", but his family was hard working and they believed in education. Robert, along with his brothers and sisters, was taught at home by his father and a few family friends. They were tutored in the evening, after they had finished working on the farm during the day. Robert was also lucky enough to attend the local school for a few months.

Robert grew up working hard on the land and reading avidly. He gained a great interest in poems and songs from his mother and his aunt, who were both well known for singing old Scots songs and retelling old Scottish tales. He first picked up the quill and wrote when he was just 15 years old, the subject of this poem was a girl, 'handsome Nell'. This innocent, but inspirational gesture, was the first of many great poems and songs that Robert would write in his lifetime.

Robert became a father at the age of 26, (with his mothers servant girl, Elizabeth Paton). He went on to have nine children with his wife, Jean Armour, and numerous other children with various different women. Farming didn't provide nearly enough of an income, so early in Robert's life he accepted an offer to become a book keeper on a plantation in Jamaica. He needed money to travel and a friend suggested that he should publish his poems to fund the trip.

A printer in Kilmarnock published his book in 1786 called, "Poems Chiefly in the Scottish Dialect". It was a success and lead to him becoming the 18th century equivalent of a "local celebrity". Robert changed his mind about going to Jamaica. He received encouragement to print another, larger, edition of his works from a leading Edinburgh critic. After borrowing a pony, he travelled to Edinburgh and within two weeks had found a printer willing to publish his larger edition. This edition was also a great success. Robert sold his rights to this book to the printer, for 100 guineas, a large sum of money at the time, but this was a decision he regretted later in life.

Robert's life then became more complicated than that of a mere tenant farmer from Ayr. He mixed with the great and the good from Edinburgh society, joined drinking and debating clubs, travelled all over Scotland and was welcomed in many stately homes. This was a very enjoyable part of Robert's life, but sadly, it didn't last for ever and he eventually found himself back working on his family farm.

Later in life Robert left farming, mainly due to ill health, and the fact that it was very hard work with little reward. He became an excise man and moved to Dumfries, taking his wife and family with him. He continued to write poetry and collect songs throughout his lifetime. He is credited with writing over 500 poems and 300 songs.

Robert Burns died on the 21st July 1796.

The name of 'Robert Burns' means different things to different people. The majority will remember poems such as "My love is like a red, red rose", "Ae fond kiss" and "Tam O' Shanter". This will conjure up images of flowers, lovers, rural Scottish landscapes and mystical beings. This is the image of Scotland's "Ploughman poet", which is only one side of Robert Burns.

There are many other aspects to Robert Burns, such as Burns the Radical; he spoke out against the hypocrisy of the church and the injustice of the class system. Burns the Revolutionary; he supported the French Revolution and the American War of Independence - both of which happened during his lifetime. Burns the Scotsman; he was fiercely proud of Scotland and a Jacobite sympathiser.

The aspect of Robert Burns that we are looking at in this book is his love of Nature. We will look at 12 works written by Robert, and examine the places, wildlife and parts of Nature that inspired him. I've also included modern English translations of the poems. These translations are here purely as an aid to understanding the original poems, as the old Scots dialect Burns used, can be difficult to understand.

1
SONG COMPOSED IN AUGUST

This song, which is a detailed depiction of autumn, draws you in close to the natural world and the emotion it contains is very convincing. This is considered by many Burns scholars to be a work of distinction, which is a little surprising, as Robert originally wrote this when he was only 17 years of age.

The version of the song printed here was written in 1783, but its origin dates back to 1775 when Robert spent a few months at a school in Kirkoswald. At the time he should have been paying attention to his studies, but he was instead paying a lot of attention to a girl called "Margaret Thomson", Known locally as "Peggy".

Margret, or Peggy as she was known, is the '*Charmer*' that Robert is '*musing*' over in this song.

The '*slaughtering guns*' mentioned in the first line refer to hunters shooting animals for food or barter. Other than the hunting of animals for food or sport, this poem portrays an enchanting autumn countryside scene full of beautiful flowers, many different types of wild birds, crops of grain ready for harvest and moonlight nights made for lovers to walk through.

Song Composed in August
By Robert Burns
Written: 1783
Type: Song
Tune: I had a horse, I had nae mair

Now westlin winds and slaught'ring guns
    Bring Autum's pleasant weather;
    The Moorcock springs on whirring wings
    Amang the blooming heather:
    Now waving grain, wide o'er the plain,
    Delights the weary farmer;
    And the moon shines bright, when I rove at night,
    To muse upon my charmer.

The partridge loves the fruitful fells,
    The plover loves the mountains;

The woodcock haunts the lonely dells,
The soaring hern the fountains:
Thro' lofty groves the Cushat roves,
The path of man to shun it;
The hazel bush o'erhangs the thrush,
The spreading thorn the linnet.

Thus ev'ry kind their pleasure find,
The savage and the tender;
Some social join, and leagues combine,
Some solitary wander:
Avaunt, away! The cruel sway,
Tyrannic man's dominion;
The sportsman's joy, the murd'ring cry,
The flutt'ring, gory pinion!

But, Peggy dear, the ev'ning's clear,
Thick flies the skimming swallow,
The sky is blue, the fields in view,
All fading-green and yellow:
Come let us stray our gladsome way,
And view the charms of nature;
The rustling corn, the fruited thorn,
And ev'ry happy creature.

We'll gently walk, and sweetly talk,
    Till the silent moon shine clearly;
    I'll grasp thy waist, and fondly prest,
    Swear how I love thee dearly:
    Not vernal show'rs to budding flow'rs,
    Not autumn to the farmer,
    So dear can be as thou to me,
    My fair, my lovely charmer!

Song Composed in August
    By Robert Burns
    Modern Translation

Now western winds and slaughtering guns
    Bring Autumn's pleasant weather;
    The Moorcock springs on whirring wings
    Among the blooming heather:
    Now waving grain, wide over the plain,
    Delights the weary farmer;
    And the moon shines bright when I walk at night,
    To think about my charmer.

The partridge loves the fruitful fells,
    The wading bird loves the mountains;
    The woodcock haunts the lonely dells,

The soaring heron the fountains:
Through lofty groves the wood pigeon roves,
The path of man to shun it;
The hazel bush overhangs the thrush,
The spreading thorn, the grey finch.

Thus every kind their pleasure find,
The savage and the tender;
Some social join, and leagues combine,
Some solitary wander:
Go Away! Away! The cruel sway,
Tyrannical man's dominion;
The sportsman's joy, the murdering cry,
The fluttering, gory wing!

But Peggy dear, the evening's clear,
Thick flies the skimming swallow,
The sky is blue, the fields in view,
All fading-green and yellow:
Come let us stray our gladsome way,
And view the charms of Nature;
The rustling corn, the fruited thorn,
And evey happy creature.

We'll gently walk, and sweetly talk,

Until the silent moon shines clearly;
I'll grab your waist, and, fondly persuaded,
Swear how I love you dearly:
Not springtime's showers to budding flowers,
Not Autumn to the farmer,
So dear can be as you to me,
My fair, my lovely charmer!

A little Extra …

An early draft of this song appears in Robert's "*First Commonplace Book*". A version of this song is also in the "*Kilmarnock edition*".

Burns revived this song later in life and included it in the book "*The Scots Musical Museum*". In this version he used more Scots language and set it to the tune "Port Gordon". This song is also in George Thomson's book, "*Select Collection of Scottish Airs*", (1799).

Robert presented Peggy, who was at that point in time married to John Neilson, (John was also a good friend of Robert's), with a copy of his Kilmarnock Edition.

The copy had the inscription, *"Once fondly lov'd, and still remembered dear"*.

2
TO A MOUSE

This is one of Robert's best-known and most recited poems. It is based on a real incident that happened at Mossgiel farm in 1785. Robert was working on the farm, ploughing a field, and accidentally destroyed a mouse's nest. When he saw what he had done, he was touched by the mouse's plight, and immediately began to write this poem. According to Robert's brother, Gilbert, he finished the poem the same day.

In this poem Robert compares the plight of the mouse with his own plight and the plight of all mankind. He shows us that no matter how well we plan we never know what's ahead of us. He goes further and suggests that the mouse is better off than us, as it can only see what is happening now, where as we can look back at depressing memories and look forward with fear and apprehension.

This is considered by scholars, and Burn's lovers, to be one of Robert's masterpieces. It has been inspiring people for over two centuries, writers, politicians, engineers, doctors, everyone from Abraham Lincoln, he was an avid Burns fan and could recite - by memory - a lot of Robert's work, to John Steinbeck, who used a quote from the poem as the title of his book, "Of Mice and Men".

When you read this poem, not only are you enjoying one of Roberts greatest pieces of work, you are also following in the footsteps of many of the world's great leaders.

To A Mouse – On Turning Her Up in Her Nest with the Plough
By Robert Burns
Written: 1785
Type: Poem

Wee, sleekit, cow'rin, tim'rous beastie,
    O, what a panic's in thy breastie!
    Thou need na start awa sae hasty,
    Wi' bickering brattle!
    I wad be laith to rin an' chase thee,

Wi' murd'ring pattle!

I'm truly sorry man's dominion,
    Has broken nature's social union,
    An' justifies that ill opinion,
    Which makes thee startle
    At me, thy poor, earth-born companion,
    An' fellow mortal!

I douibt na, whiles, but thou may thieve;
    What then? Poor beastie, thou maun live!
    A daimen icker in a thrave
    's a sma' request;
    I'll get a blessin wi' the lave,
    An never miss't!

Thy wee bit housie, too, in ruin!
    It's silly wa's the win's are strewin!
    An' naething, now, to big a new ane,
    O' foggage green!
    An' bleak December's winds ensuing,
    Baith snell an' keen!

Thou saw the fields laid bare an' waste,

An' weary winter comin fast,
An' cozie here, beneath the blast,
Thou thought to dwell,
Till crash! The cruel coulter past
Out thro' thy cell.

That wee bit heap o' leaves an' stibble,
Has cost thee mony a weary nibble!
Now thou's turn'd out, for a' thy trouble,
But house or hald,
To thole the winter's sleety dribble
An' cranreuch cauld !

But, Mousie, thou art no thy lane,
In proving foresight may be in vain;
The best laid schemes o' mice an' men
Gang aft agley,
An' lea'e us nought but grief an' pain,
For promis'd joy!

Still thou art blest, compar'd wi' me
The present only toucheth thee:
But, Och! I backward cast my e'e,
On prospects drear!
An' forward, tho' I canna see,

I guess an' fear!

To A Mouse – On Turning Her Up in Her Nest with the Plough
By Robert Burns
MODERN TRANSLATION

Small, sneaky, cowering, fearful animal,
Oh, what a panic is in your heart!
You need not run away so quickly,
With argumentative chatter!
I would be loathed to run and chase you,
With a murdering plough handle!

I'm truly sorry man's dominion,
Has broken nature's social union,
And justifies that bad opinion,
Which makes you jump with fright
At me, your poor, earth-born companion,
And fellow-mortal!

I doubt not, at times, you may steal;
What then? Poor animal, you must live!
An odd ear of corn in a bundle of 24

Is a small request;
I'll get a blessing with what is left,
And never miss it !

Your small house, too, in ruin!
It's silly walls the winds are blowing away!
And nothing, now, to build a new one,
No grass that's green
And bleak Decembers winds are coming,
Both bitter and sharp!

You saw the fields laid bare and waste,
And weary winter coming fast,
And comfortable here, beneath the blast,
You thought to dwell,
Until crash ! the cruel plough blade past
Out through your small house.

That small heap of leaves, grass and hay,
Has cost you many a weary nibble!
Now you're thrown out, for all your trouble,
Without house or property,
To suffer the winter's sleety dribble,
And frosty cold!

But mouse, you are not alone,
> *In proving foresight may be vain:*
> *The best laid schemes of Mice and Men*
> *Often go wrong,*
> *And leave us nothing but grief and pain,*
> *Instead of promised joy!*

Still, you are blessed, compared with me!
> *The present only touches you:*
> *But oh! I backward cast my eye,*
> *On prospects bleak!*
> *And forward, though I cannot see,*
> *I guess and fear!*

A Little Extra …

There are a lot of similarities between the theme's in this poem and Adam Smith's book, 'The Theory of Moral Sentiments' (1759), which was a key text in the moral philosophy of the "Scottish Enlightenment Movement".

3
ON SCARING SOME WATER-FOWEL

In 1787, at the age of 28, Robert was beginning to prosper. His second edition of poems was selling very well and this gave him both money and fame. He decided to capitalise on this new fame and went on several tours around Scotland. He made a point of visiting the gentry and noblemen, i.e. the cream of society. 18th century poets depended on patronage from the great and the wealthy, so this was Robert engaging in a bit of salesmanship.

During one of his tours, in the autumn of 1787, Robert was a guest of Sir William Murray of Ochtertyre, in Perthshire. It was during his stay here that he wrote: *"On Scaring some Watwer-Fowel in Loch Turit"*.

This poem has many of the same themes as *"To A Mouse"*. It highlights the broken union between man and Nature, while showing us some of the life and habitats of wild birds. This also highlights man's pompous attitude to Nature and points out the perverse pleasure we get from the pain and killing of animals. This killing is usually done in the name of "country sports" and "country life".

On Scaring some Water-Fowel in Loch Turit

By Robert Burns
Written: 1787
Type: Poem

Why, ye tenants of the lake,
> For me your wat'ry haunt forsake?
> Tell me, fellow creatures, why
> At my presence thus you fly?
> Why disturb your social joys,
> Parent filial, kindred ties?

Common friend to you and me,
> Nature's gifts to all are free:
> Peaceful keep your dimpling wave,
> Busy feed, or wanton lave;
> Or beneath the sheltering rock,
> Bide the surging billow's shock.

Conscious, blushing for our race,
    Soon, too soon, your fears I trace,
    Man, your proud, unsurping foe,
    Would be lord of all below:
    Plumes himself in freedom's pride,
    Tyrant stern to all beside.

The eagle, from the ciffy brow,
    Marking you his prey below,
    In his breast no pity dwells,
    Strong necessity compels:
    But Man, to whom alone is given
    A ray direct from pitying heaven,
    Glories in his heart humane,
    And all creatures for his pleasure slain!

In these savage, liquid plains,
    Only known to wand'ring swains,
    Where the mossy riv'let strays,
    Far from human haunts and ways;
    All on Nature you depend,
    And life's poor season peaceful spend.

Or, if man's superior might
    Dare invade your native right,

On the lofty ether borne,
Man with all his pow'rs you scorn;
Swiftly seek, on clanging wings,
Other lakes and other springs;
And the foe you cannot brave,
Scorn at least to be his slave.

On Scaring Some Water-Fowl in Loch Turit
By Robert Burns
Modern Translation

Why, you tenants of the lake,
For me your watery haunts forsake?
Tell me, fellow-creatures, why
At my presence thus you fly?
Why disturb your social joys,
Parent, dutiful, family ties?

Common friend to you and me,
Nature's gifts to all are free:
Peaceful keep your undulating wave,
Busy feed, before willful washing
Or, beneath the sheltering rock
Endure the surging billow's shock.

Conscious, blushing for our race,
  Soon, too soon, your fears I trace,
  Man, your proud, usurping foe,
  Would be lord of all below:
  Displays himself in freedom's pride,
  Tyrant stern to all beside.

The eagle, from the cliffy brow,
  Marking you his prey below,
  In his breast no pity dwells,
  Strong necessity compels:
  Without Man, to whom alone is given,
  A ray direct from pitying Heaven,
  Glories in his heart humane,
  And creatures for his pleasure slain!

In these savage, liquid plains,
  Only known to wandering lovers,
  Where the mossy riv'let strays,
  Far from human haunts and ways;
  All on nature you depend,
  And life's poor season peaceful spend.

Or, if man's superior might
  Dare invade your native right,

On the lofty ether borne,
Man with all his powers you scorn;
Swiftly seek, on clanging wings,
Other lakes and other springs;
And the foe you cannot brave,
Scorn at least to be his slave.

A little Extra …

Robert wrote this poem in one day while out walking from Oughtertyre House. We know this as there is a note, in his own hand writing, on the *"Glenriddell Manuscript"* that says:

"This was the production of a solitary forenoon's walk from Oughtertyre House. I lived there, the guest of Sir William Murray, for two or three weeks, and was much flattered by my hospitable reception."

According to one of Sir William Murray's cousins, (who was staying at Oughertyre House at the same time as Burns), Robert recited the poem after supper one evening.

This poem was first published in *"The Edinburgh Edition"* in 1793.

Loch Turret, (which is just above the town of Crieff), has changed a lot since Robert's visit in 1787. The Glen has been dammed to create a much larger reservoir; this has unfortunately taken away a lot of the habitat for birds.

4
ADMIRING NATURE IN HER WILDEST GRACE

This poem was written by Burns while on his tour of the highlands in 1787. It is said that he composed it whilst standing on a small bridge on the outskirts of the town of Kenmore. He had travelled from Crieff and paid a visit to Taymouth Castle before staying at the Inn at Kenmore.

Taymouth Castle was the seat of the Campbell's of Breadalbane. At the time of Burn's visit it was the home of John Campbell, Earl of Breadalbane, (1762 – 1834).

He also wrote a copy of the poem in pencil on the chimney-piece of the Inn.

Verses written with a pencil over the Chimney-Piece in the Parlour of the Inn at Kenmore, Taymouth
By Robert Burns

Written: 1787

Type: Poem

Admiring Nature in her wildest grace,
 These northern scenes with weary feet I trace;
 O'er many a winding dale and painful steep,
 Th' abodes of cove'd grouse and timid sheep,

My savage journey, curious, I pursue,
 Till fam'd Breadalbane opens to my view.
 The meeting cliffs each deep-sunk glen divides,
 The woods wild scatter'd clothe their ample sides;
 Th' outstretching lake, imbosomed 'mong the hills,
 The eye with wonder and amazement fills;
 The Tay meand'ring sweet in infant pride,
 The palace rising on his verdant side,
 The lawns wood-fring'd in Nature's native taste,
 The hillocks dropt in Nature's careless haste,
 The arches striding o'er the new-born stream,
 The village glittering in the noontide beam.

Poetic ardours in my bosom swell,
 Lone wand'ring by the hermit's mossy cell;
 The sweeping theatre of hanging woods,

Th' incessant roar of headlong tumbling floods.

Here Poesy might wake her heav'n-taught lyre,
    And look through Nature with creative fire;
    Here, to the wrongs of Fate half reconcil'd,
    Misfortunes lighten'd steps might wander wild;
    And disappointment, in these lonely bounds,
    Find balm to sooth her bitter, rankling wounds:
    Here heart-struck grief might heav'nward stretch her.
    And injured worth forget and pardon man.

Verses written with a pencil over the Chimney-Piece in the Parlour of the Inn at Kenmore, Taymouth
    By Robert Burns
    Modern Translation

Admiring Nature in her wildest grace,
    These northern scenes with weary feet I trace;
    Over many a winding dale and painful steep,
    The homes of families of grouse and timid sheep,

My savage journey, curious, I pursue,
    Till famed Breadalbane opens to my view.

The meeting cliffs, each deep-sunk glen divides,
The woods wild scattered, clothe their ample sides;
The outstretching lake, imbedded among the hills,
The eye with wonder and amazement fills;
The Tay meandering sweet in infant pride,
The palace rising on his lush side,
The lawns wood-fringed in Nature's native taste,
The hillocks dropt in Nature's careless haste,
The arches striding over the new-born stream,
The village glittering in the noontide beam.

Poetic passions in my heart swell,
Lone wandering beside the hermit's mossy cell;
The sweeping theatre of hanging woods,
The incessant roar of headlong tumbling floods.

Her Poesy might wake her heaven-taught instrument,
And look through Nature with creative fire;
Here, to the wrongs of Fate half reconciled,
Misfortunes lightened steps might wander wild;
And disappointment, in these lonely bounds,
Find balm to soothe her bitter, festering wounds:
Here heart-struck Grief might heavenward stretch her
And injured worth forget and pardon man.

A little Extra …

This poem is also referred to as, "*Written in the Hermitage at Taymouth*"

Breadalbane was immortalized in another one of Burn's works, "*Address of Beelzebub*"

Both the Inn, now called "*The Kenmore Hotel*", and the hand written poem survive to this day. The chimney, and hand written poem, are located in a part of the hotel that's now called, "*The Poet's Bar*".

5

THE BIRKS OF ABERFELDY

T his song was written in August 1787 during Burns tour of the highlands. At this point He has reached Perthshire and the town of Aberfeldy. During a walk around the outskirts of the town Burns sees some Birch trees and is inspired by the beauty of the scenery to write this song.

On the manuscript copy of the song there is a note in Burns own handwriting telling us that the song was "*composed on the spot*".

This is primarily a love song but it also describes the beautiful woodland scenery around Aberfeldy. Burns would have had to use a little imagination as he writes as though it is summertime, but he was there in late August.

The Birks of Aberfeldy
    By Robert Burns
    Written: 1787

Type: Song
Tune: The Birks of Aberfeldy

Chorus

    Bonie lassie, will ye go,
    Will ye go, will ye go,
    Bonie lassie, will ye go
    To the birks of Aberfeldy

Now Simmer blinks on flowery braes,
    And o'er the crystal streamlets plays;
    Come let us spend the lightsome days,
    In the birks of Aberfeldy.

Chorus

    Bonie lassie, will ye go,
    Will ye go, will ye go,
    Bonie lassie, will ye go
    To the birks of Aberfeldy

While o'er their heads the hazels hing,
    The little birdies blithely sing,
    Or lightly flit on wanton wing,
    In the birks of Aberfeldy.

Chorus

    Bonie lassie, will ye go,
    Will ye go, will ye go,
    Bonie lassie, will ye go
    To the birks of Aberfeldy

The braes ascend like lofty wa's,
    The foaming stream deep-roaring fa's,
    O'erhung wi' fragrant spreading shaws,
    The birks of Aberfeldy.

Chorus

    Bonie lassie, will ye go,
    Will ye go, will ye go,
    Bonie lassie, will ye go
    To the birks of Aberfeldy

The hoary cliffs are crown'd wi flowers,
    White o'er the linns the burnie pours,
    And rising, weets wi' misty showers,
    The birks of Aberfeldy.

Chorus

    Bonie lassie, will ye go,

    Will ye go, will ye go,

    Bonie lassie, will ye go

    To the birks of Aberfeldy

Let fortune's gift at randoe flee,

    They ne'er shall draw a wish frae me;

    Supremely blest wi' love and thee,

    In the birks of Aberfeldy.

Chorus

    Bonie lassie, will ye go,

    Will ye go, will ye go,

    Bonie lassie, will ye go

    To the birks of Aberfeldy

The Birks of Aberfeldy

    By Robert Burns

    Modern Translation

Chorus

    Beautiful girl, will you go,

    Will you go, will you go,

Beautiful girl, will you go,
To the birches of Aberfeldy

Now summer blinks on flowery hillsides,
And over the crystal streamlets plays;
Come let us spend the carefree days,
In the birches of Aberfeldy.

Chorus
Beautiful girl, will you go,
Will you go, will you go,
Beautiful girl, will you go,
To the birches of Aberfeldy

While over their heads the hazels hang,
The little birds happily sing,
Before lightly moving on frolicking wing,
In the birches of Aberfeldy.

Chorus
Beautiful girl, will you go,
Will you go, will you go,
Beautiful girl, will you go,
To the birches of Aberfeldy

36

The hillsides ascend like lofty walls,
    The foaming stream deep-roaring falls,
    Overhung with fragrant spreading trees,
    The birches of Aberfeldy.

Chorus
    Beautiful girl, will you go,
    Will you go, will you go,
    Beautiful girl, will you go,
    To the birches of Aberfeldy

The greyish cliffs are crowned with flowers,
    White, over the waterfalls the stream pours,
    And rising, joins with misty showers,
    In the birches of Aberfeldy.

Chorus
    Beautiful girl, will you go,
    Will you go, will you go,
    Beautiful girl, will you go,
    To the birches of Aberfeldy

Let fortune's gifts at random flee,
  They never shall draw a wish from me;
  Supremely blest with love and you,
  In the birches of Aberfeldy.

Chorus
  Beautiful girl, will you go,
  Will you go, will you go,
  Beautiful girl, will you go,
  To the birches of Aberfeldy

A little Extra ...

"*Birks*" is a Scottish word for "*Birch Trees*"

Whilst here Burns also visited "*The Falls of Acharn*", this is a large waterfall to the west of Aberfeldy, near Loch Tay.

There is now a statue of Burns in the 'Birks of Aberfeldy'. The statue is of him sitting on a bench, writing.

6

CASTLE GORDON

Robert wrote this poem on the 7th September 1787, during his tour of the highlands.

Robert had previously met the Duchess of Gordon in Edinburgh, and as a result of that meeting, he was invited to visit the Duke and Duchess at Castle Gordon. The castle, which during the 18th century was reputed to be the largest building in Scotland, is situated just outside the town of Fochabers.

Robert definitely enjoyed his time here and wrote in his journal about the visit.

"fine palace worthy of the noble, the polite, the generous Proprietor – Dine – Company, Duke & Duchess & Ladies charlotte & Magdeline - The Duke Makes me happier than ever great man did – noble princely yet mild condescending and affable gay & kind – The Duchess charming witty kind and sensible, God Bless Them."

The poem was written as a tribute to the Duke and Duchess.

Castle Gordon
    By Robert Burns
    Written : 1787
    Type : Poem

Streams that glide in orient plains,
    Never bound by winter's chains;
    Glowing here on golden sands,
    From tyranny's empurpled hands;
    These, their richly gleaming waves,
    I leave to tyrants and their slaves;
    Give me the stream that sweetly laves
    The banks by Castle Gordon.

Spicy forests, ever gray,
    Shading from the burning ray
    Hapless wretches sold to toil;
    Or the ruthless native's way,
    Bent on slaughter, blood, and spoil:
    Woods that ever verdant wave,
    I leave the tyrant and the slave;
    Give me the groves that lofty brave

The storms by Castle Gordon.

Wildly here, without control,
    Nature reigns and rules the whole;
    In that sober pensive mood,
    Dearest to the feeling soul,
    She plants the forest, pours the flood:
    Life's poor day I'll musing rave
    And find at night a sheltering cave,
    Where waters flow and wild woods wave,
    By bonie Castle Gordon.

Castle Gordon
    By Robert Burns
    Modern Translation

Streams that glide in orient plains,
    Never bound by winter's chains;
    Glowing here on golden sands,
    There intermixed with foulest stains
    From tyranny's empurpled hands;
    These, their richly gleaming waves,
    I leave to tyrants and their slaves;
    Give me the stream that sweetly washes
    The banks by Castle Gordon.

Spicy forests, ever gray,
  Shading from the burning ray
  Unfortunate wretches sold to toil;
  Before the ruthless native's way,
  Bent on slaughter, blood, and spoil:
  Woods that ever leafy wave,
  I leave the tyrant and the slave;
  Give me the groves that lofty brave
  The storms by Castle Gordon.

Wildly here, without control,
  Nature reigns and rules the whole;
  In that sober thoughtful mood,
  Dearest to the feeling soul,
  She plants the forest, pours the flood:
  Life's poor day I'll thinking rave
  And find at night a sheltering cave,
  By beautiful Castle Gordon.

A Little Extra …

Robert would probably have stayed longer at Castle
Gordon but his travelling companion, William Nicol,

urged him to leave. William did this as he was angry that had not been invited to dine at the Castle and had been left behind at an inn. Robert wrote out a copy of the poem and gave it to the Dukes librarian, along with a letter of apology over his quick departure.

7

THE HUMBLE PETITION OF BRIAR WATER

This poem was written in 1787 during Robert's Highland tour. He was on his way north when he stopped and visited Blair Castle. The Falls of Bruar are a few miles north West of the town of Blair Atholl.

This poem is addressed to the Duke of Atholl, and it is meant as an introduction from Robert to the Duke with the hope that the Duke would become one of Robert's patrons, i.e. Robert was engaging in a bit of salesmanship, or social climbing.

In the poem itself Roberts imagines that he is the "Bruar Water" and he asks the Duke to plant trees along his banks. The Duke would be rewarded by walking under their shade and hear the song from birds nesting in their branches.

There is a footnote in Roberts journal on the day he visited Bruar Falls. It says:

"Bruar Falls, in Athole, are exceedingly picturesque and beautiful; but their effect is much impaired by the want of trees and shrubs. – R.B."

The Humble Petition of Bruar Water

By Robert Burns
Written: 1787
Type: Poem

My lord, I know your noble ear
    Woe ne'er assails in vain;
    Embolden'd thus, I beg you'll hear
    Your humble slave complain,
    How saucy Phoebus' scorching beams,
    In flaming summer-pride,
    Dry-withering, waste my foamy streams,
    And drink my crystal tide.

The lightly-jumping, glowrin' trouts,
    That thro' my waters play,
    If, in their random, wanton spouts,
    They near the margin stray;
    If, hapless chance! They linger lang,

I'm scorching up so shallow,
They're left the whitening stanes amang,
In gasping death to wallow.

Last day I grat wi' spite and teen,
    As poet Burns came by.
    That, to a bard, I should be seen
    Wi' half my channel dry;
    A panegyric rhyme, I ween,
    Ev'n as I was, he shor'd me;
    But had I in my glory been,
    He, kneeling, wad ador'd me.

Here foaming down the skelvy rocks,
    In twisting strength I rin;
    There, high my boiling torrent smokes,
    Wild-roaring o'er a linn:
    Enjoying each large spring and well,
    As Nature gave them me,
    I am, altho' I say't mysel',
    Worth gaun a mile to see.

Would then my noble master please
    To grant my highest wishes,
    He'll shade my banks wi' tow'rinng trees,

And bonie spreading bushes.
Delighted doubly then, my lord,
You'll wander on my banks,
And listen mony a grateful bird
Return you tuneful thanks.

The sober lav'rock, warbling wild,
  Shall to the skirs aspire;
  The gowdspink, music's gayest child,
  Shall sweetly join the choir;
  The blackbird strong, the lintwhite clear,
  The mavis mild and mellow;
  The robin pensive Autumn cheer,
  In all her locks of yellow.

This, too, a covert shall ensure,
  To shield them from the storm;
  And coward maukin sleep secure,
  Low in her grassy form:
  Here shall the shepherd make his seat,
  To weave his crown of flow'rs;
  Or find a shelt'ring, safe retreat,
  From prone-descending show'rs.

And here, by sweet, endearing stealth,

Shall meet the loving pair,
Despising worlds, with all their wealth,
As empty idle care;
The flow'rs shall vie in all their charms,
The hour of heav'n to grace;
And birks extend their fragrant arms
To screen the dear embrace.

Here haply too, at vernal dawn,
Some musing bard may stray,
And eye the smoking, dewy lawn,
And misty mountain grey;
Or, by the reaper's nightly beam,
Mild-chequering thro' the trees,
Rave to my darkly dashing stream,
Hoarse-swelling on the breeze.

Let lofty firs, and ashes cool,
My lowly banks o'erspread,
And view, deep-bending in the pool,
Their shadow's wat'ry bed:
Let fragrant birks, in woodbines drest,
My craggy cliffs adorn;
And, for the little songster's nest,
The close embow'ring thorn.

So may old Scotia's darling hope,
    Your little angel band
    Spring, like their fathers, up to prop,
    Their honour'd native land!
    So may, thro' Albion's farthest ken,
    To social-flowing glasses,
    The grace be – Athole's honest men,
    And Athole's bonie lasses!

The Humble Petition of Bruar Water
    By Robert Burns
    Modern Translation

My lord, I know your noble ear
    Woe never disturbs in vain
    With new confidence, I beg you'll hear
    Your humble slave complain,
    How saucy sunshine's scorching beams,
    In flaming summer-pride,
    Dry-withering, waste my foamy streams,
    And drink my crystal tide.

The lightly-jumping, angry-looking trouts,
    That through my waters play,
    If, in their random, willful spouts,

They near the margin stray;
If, hapless chance! They linger long,
I'm scorching up so shallow,
They are left the whitening stones among,
In gasping death to wallow.

Last day I wept with spite and sorrow,
As poet Burns came by.
That, to a bard, I should be seen
With half my channel dry;
A testimonial rhyme, I guess,
Even as I was, he threatened me;
But had I in my glory been,
He, kneeling, would have adored me.

Here, foaming down the layered rocks,
In twisting strength I run;
There, high my boiling torrent smokes,
Wild-roaring over a waterfall:
Enjoying each large spring and well,
As Nature gave them me,
I am, although I say it myself,
Worth going a mile to see.

Would then my noble master please

To grant my highest wishes,
He'll shade my banks with towering trees,
And beautiful spreading bushes.
Delighted doubly then, my lord,
You'll wander on my banks,
And listen to many a grateful bird
Return you tuneful thanks.

The sober skylark, warbling wild,
Shall to the skies aspire;
The Goldfinch, music's gayest child,
Shall sweetly join the choir;
The blackbird strong, the finch clear,
The thrush mild and yellow;
The robin pensive Autumn cheer,
In all her locks of yellow.

This, too, a hiding place shall ensure,
To shield them from the storm;
And snug a hare sleep secure,
Low in her grassy form:
Here shall the shepard make his seat,
To weave his crown of flowers;
Or find a sheltering, safe retreat,
From prone-descending showers.

And here, by sweet, endearing stealth,
    Shall meet the loving pair,
    Despising worlds, with all their wealth,
    As empty idle care;
    The flowers shall compete in all their charms,
    The hour of heaven to grace;
    And trees extend their fragrant arms
    To screen the dear embrace.

Here perhaps too, at springtime's dawn,
    Some musing bard may stray
    And eye the smoking, dewy lawn,
    And misty mountain grey;
    Or, by the reaper's nightly beam,
    Mild-chequering through the trees,
    Rave to my darkly dashing stream,
    Hoarse-swelling on the breeze.

Let lofty firs, and ashes cool,
    My lowly banks overspread,
    And view, deep-bendingin the pool,
    Their shadow's watery bed:
    Let fragrent trees, in woodbines dressed,
    My craggy cliffs adorn;
    And, for the little sogster's nest,
    The close surrounding thorn.

So may old Scotland's darling hope,
  Your little angel band
  Spring, like their fathers, up to prop
  Their honoured native land !
  So may, through Albion's farthest Knowledge,
  To social-flowing glasses,
  The grace be "Athole's honest men,
  And Athole's beautiful lasses!

A Little Extra ...

While staying at Blair Castle Robert met a gentleman called 'Graham of Fintry''. Graham became a very loyal and influential friend.

Robert would probably have stayed longer at Blair Castle, but again, his traveling companion, Willie Nicol, made him move on. This is probably because Willie was angry / jealous that he was not invited to the castle.

The banks of the Falls of Bruar have now been planted with trees. There are also two bridges and a path, which leads visitors around the most picturesque areas of the falls. I believe The Bard would approve.

8

UP IN THE MORNING EARLY - (WINTER)

This song was written by Robert in 1788, probably at Ellisland farm, which is close to the town of Dumfries.

Judging by the sentiment in this song he didn't always relish the prospect of getting up early and working in the cold and snow! It's the kind of song that makes you want to stay in bed and enjoy the warmth under the duvet.

Up in the Morning Early – (Winter)
   By Robert Burns
   Written: 1788
   Type: Song

Cauld blaws the wind frae east to west,
   The drift is driving sairly;
   Sae loud and shill's I hear the blast,
   I'm sure it's winter fairly.

Chorus

    Up in the mornings no for me,
    Up in the morning early;
    When a' the hills are covered wi' snaw,
    I'm sure it's winter fairly.

The birds sit chittering in the thorn,
    A' day they fare but sparely:
    And langs the night frae e'en to morn,
    I'm sure its winter fairly.

Chorus

    Up in the mornings no for me,
    Up in the morning early;
    When a' the hills are covered wi' snaw,
    I'm sure it's winter fairly.

Up in the morning early
    By Robert Burns
    Modern Translation

Cold blows the wind from east to west,

The drift is driving sorely;
So loud and piercing I hear the blast,
I'm sure it's winter fairly.

Chorus

Up in the morning is not for me,
Up in the morning early;
When all the hills are covered with snow,
I'm sure its winter fairly.

The birds sit shivering in the thorn,
All day they fare but sparsely
And long is the night, from evening to morning,
I'm sure it's winter fairly.

Chorus

Up in the morning is not for me,
Up in the morning early;
When all the hills are covered with snow,
I'm sure its winter fairly.

A little Extra …

Robert knew that farming was hard work and wasn't always profitable so he started training as an excise man. This proved to be a wise decision.

Robert didn't always dislike the winter, as this excerpt from his Common-Place book shows:

"There is scarcely any earthly object gives me more – I don't know if I should call it pleasure, but something which exults me, something which enraptures me – than to walk in the sheltered side of a wood or high plantation, in a cloudy, winter day, and hear a stormy wind howling among the trees and raving o'er the plain. – It is my best season for devotion. "

(First Common-Place Book April 1784)

This is the year that Robert wrote "Auld Lang Syne".

9

THE WOUNDED HARE

This poem was written by Robert in 1789. It is based on an actual shooting, which took place in the fields at Ellisland Farm.

He mentions the event in a letter he wrote to his friend, "Mrs Dunlop", dated the 21st of April 1789:

"While sowing in the fields, I heard a shot, and presently a poor little hare limped by me, apparently very much hurt. ... this set my humanity in tears..."

This shooting obviously upset and angered Robert. This can be easily seen in the tone of the poem, which is very hostile to the hunter. He also thinks about the cruel fate of the hare and the effect it has on its family.

The "Nith" is a river in the south west of Scotland.

The Wounded Hare

By Robert Burns
Written : 1789
Type : Poem

Inhuman man! curse on thy barb'rous art,
    And blasted be thy murder-aiming eye;
    May never pity soothe thee with a sigh,
    Nor ever pleasure glad thy cruel heart!

Go live, poor wand'rer of the wood and field!
    The bitter little that life remains:
    No more the thickening brakes and verdant plains
    To thee a home, or food, or pastime yield.

Seek, mangled wretch,some place of wonted rest,
    No more of rest, but now thy dying bed!
    The sheltering rushes whistling o'er thy head,
    The cold earth with thy bloody bosom prest.

Perhaps a mother's anguish adds its woe;
    The playful crowd fondly by thy side;
    Ah! Helpless nurslings, who will now provide
    That life a mother only can bestow!

Oft as by winding Nith I, musing, wait

The sober eve, or hail the cheerful dawn,

I'll miss thee sporting o'er the dewy lawn,

And curse the ruffian's aim, and mourn thy hapless fate.

The Wounded hare
By Robert Burns
Modern Translation

Inhuman man! Curse on your barbarous art,
And blasted be your murder-aiming eye;
May never pity soothe you with a sigh,
Nor ever pleasure glad your cruel heart!

Go live, poor wanderer of the wood and field!
The bitter little that of life remains:
No more the thickening brakes and verdant plains
To you a home, or food, or pastime yield.

Look, mangled wretch, for some place of wanted rest.
No more rest, but now your dying bed!
The sheltering rushes whistling over your head,
The cold earth with your bloody bosom prest.

Perhaps a mother's anguish adds its sorrow;
    The playful pair crowd fondly by your side;
    Ah! Helpless nurslings, who will now provide
    That life a mother only can give!

Often as by winding nith I, thinking, wait
    The sober evening, before the cheerful dawn,
    I'll miss you sporting over the dewy lawn,
    And curse the ruffian's aim, and mourn your
hapless fate.

A Little Extra …

The *"Inhuman man!"* mentioned in the poem, i.e. the hunter who shot the hare, was actually a young man called "Thomson". We believe this to be true as there was an account of the event, which was written by a gentleman after he met him:

"This poem is founded on fact. A young man of the name of Thomson told me – quite unconscious of the existence of the poem – that while Burns lived at

Ellisland – he shot and hurt a hare, which in the twilight was feeding on his fathers wheat-bread. The poet, on observing the hare come bleeding past him, "was in great wrath," said Thomson, "and cursed me, and said little hindered him from throwing me into the Nith; and he was able enough to do it, though I was both young and strong."

An early version of this poem was found at Floors Castle, Roxburghshire, in 2011. The manuscript was enclosed in a letter dated 17th May 1789.

10

THE GARDNER WI' HIS PAIDLE

This song / poem was written by Robert in 1789. The title has been taken from an older song, but the verses are attributed him.

In this song / poem Robert uses great natural imagery to show the rural landscape at its best. It paints the picture of a happy Gardner working outside during the day and then going home to the loving arms of is wife / sweetheart.

A "Paidle" is a long handled tool used for weeding / scraping.

The Gard'ner wi' his Paidle
By Robert Burns
Written: 1789
Type: Song / Poem
Tune: The Gardener's March

When rosy May comes in wi' flowers,
    To deck her gay, green-spreading bowers,
    Then busy, busy are his hours,
    The Gard'ner wi' his paidle.

The crystal waters gently fa',
    The merry bards are lovers a',
    The scented breezes round him blaw –
    The Gard'ner wi' his paidle.

When purple morning starts the hare
    To steal upon her early fare;
    Then thro' the dews he maun repair –
    The Gard'ner wi' his paidle.

When day, expiring in the west,
    The curtain draws o' nature's rest,
    He flies to her arms he lo'es the best,
    The Gard'ner wi' his paidle.

The Gard'ner wi' his paidle
    By Robert Burns
    Modern Translation

When rosy May comes in with flowers,
    To deck her gay, green-spreading shade,
    Then busy, busy are his hours,
    The Gardener with his weeder.

The crystal waters gently fall,
    The merry birds are lovers all,
    The scented breezes around him blow –
    The Gardener with his weeder.

When purple morning starts the hare
    To steal upon her early fare;
    Then through the dews he must go –
    The Gardener with his weeder.

When day, expiring in the west,
    The curtain draws over nature's rest,
    He flies to her arms he loves the best,
    The Gardner with his weeder.

A Little Extra …

This poem / song was published in James Johnson's "Scots Musical Museum" in 1790.

In this year, (1789), Robert and Jean Armour had another child, "Francis Wallace Burns"

11

BY ALLAN STREAM

This poem / song was written by Robert in 1793. This is getting towards the last few years of Roberts life and at this stage he is becoming more and more unwell.

At this point in time Robert had left farming behind and is living with his family in Dumfries. Despite his ill health he continues to work as an excise officer and in his spare time collect and write songs for George Thomson's book, "Scots Musical Museum."

This song / poem is mentioned in a letter from Robert to George Thomson dated the 19th August 1793, in it he wrote:

"I walked out yesterday evening with a volume of the Museum in my hand, when turning up 'Allan Water'… It appeared to me rather unworthy of so fine an air: and recollecting that it is on your list, I sat, and raved, under the shade of an old thorn, till I

wrote one to suit the measure. I may be wrong; but I think it not my worst style."

This is a beautiful song / poem about two lovers meeting in the luscious rural landscape by Allan Stream. It is no wonder Robert liked this piece, as it is not only well written, but may well have reminded him of his days as a younger, healthier man.

By Allan Stream

By Robert Burns
Written: 1793
Type: Song / Poem
Tune: Allan Water

By Allan stream I chanc'd to rove,
    While Phoebus sank beyond Ben Ledi;
    The winds are whispering thro' the grove,
    The yellow corn was waving ready:
    I listen'd to a lover's sang,
    An' though on youthfu' pleasures mony;
    And aye the wild-wood echoes rang –
    "O, dearly do I love thee, Annie!

"O, happy be thee woodbine bower,
    Nae nightly bogle make it eerie;
    Nor ever sorrow stain the hour,
    The place and time I met my dearie!
    Her head upon my throbbing breast,
    She, sinking, said, 'I'm thine for ever!'
    While mony a kiss the seal imprest –
    The sacred vow we ne'er should sever.

The haunt o' Springs the primrose-brae
    The summer joys the floks to follow;
    How cheery through her short'ning day,
    Is Autumn in her weeds o' yellow;
    But can they melt the glowing heart,
    Or chain the soul in speechless pleasure?
    Or thro' each nerve the rapture dart,
    Like meeting her, our bosom's treasure?

By Allan Stream
    By Robert Burns
    Modern Translation

By Allan stream I chanced to walk,
    While the sun sank beyond Ben Ledi;
    The winds are whispering through the grove,

The yellow corn was waving ready:
I listened to a lover's song,
And thought on youthful pleasures many;
And all the wild-wood echoes rang,
O, dearly do I love thee, Annie!

O, happy be the woodbine plant,
  No nightly demon make it eerie;
  Nor ever sorrow stain the hour,
  The place and time I met my Dearie!
  Her head upon my throbbing breast,
  She, sinking, said, "I'm yours for ever!"
  While many a kiss the seal impressed
  The sacred vow we never should sever.

The haunt o' Spring's the primrose-hillside,
  The Summer joys the flocks to follow;
  How cheery through her shortening day,
  Is Autumn in her weeds of yellow;
  But can they melt the glowing heart,
  Or chain the soul in speechless pleasure?
  Or through each nerve the rapture dart,
  Like meeting her, our heart's treasure?

A Little Extra …

Allan Water is a river, which can be found throughout Strathallan, Perthsire.

Ben Ledi is a large hill just outside of the town of Callander, which is in the Trossachs.

12

CA' THE YOWES TO THE KNOWES

This is the second version of 'Ca'the Yowes to the knowes", Robert wasn't happy with his first attempt, this version was written in 1794. He kept the chorus from the original, but has written completely new verses.

It is believed that he produced this version *"while on a solitary evening stroll in September 1794."*

This is a beautiful rural love song, which describes two people living and working together, tending their sheep. Robert also indulges in a little 18th century supernatural folklore, in verses three and four, when he mentions Fairies, Ghost's and Bogle's.

The "Clouden" is a tributary of the river Nith.

"Clouden's silent towers" are the ruins of Lincluden Abbey.

Ca' The Yowes to the Knowes

By Robert Burns
(Second Version)
Written: 1794
Type: Song / Poem
Tune: ?

Chorus

Ca' the yowes to the knowes,
Ca' them where the heather grows,
Ca' them where the burnie rowes,
My bonie dearie.

Hark the mavis' e'ening sang,
Sounding Clouden's woods amang;
Then a-faulding let us gang,
My bonie dearie.

Chorus

Ca' the yowes to the knowes,
Ca' them where the heather grows,
Ca' them where the burnie rowes,
My bonie dearie.

We'll gae down by Clouden side,
  Thro' the Hazels, spreading wide,
  O'er the waves that sweetly glide,
  To the moon sae clearly.

Chorus
  Ca' the yowes to the knowes,
  Ca' them where the heather grows,
  Ca' them where the burnie rowes,
  My bonie dearie.

Yonder Clouden's silent towers,
  Where, at moonshine's midnight hours,
  O'er the dewy-bending flowers,
  Faries dance sae cheery.

Chorus
  Ca' the yowes to the knowes,
  Ca' them where the heather grows,
  Ca' them where the burnie rowes,
  My bonie dearie.

Ghaist nor bogle shalt thou fear,
    Thou'rt to love an Heav'n sae dear,
    Nocht of ill may come thee near;
    My bonie dearie.

Chorus
    Ca' the yowes to the knowes,
    Ca' them where the heather grows,
    Ca' them where the burnie rowes,
    My bonie dearie.

Fair and lovely as thou art,
    Thou hast stown my very heart;
    I can die, but canna part,
    My bonie dearie.

Chorus
    Ca' the yowes to the knowes,
    Ca' them where the heather grows,
    Ca' them where the burnie rowes,
    My bonie dearie.

Ca' The Yowes To The Knowes
    By Robert Burns

(Second Version)

Chorus
 Drive the sheep to the hills,
 Drive them where the heather grows,
 Drive them where the stream rolls,
 My beautiful darling.

Listen to the Thrush's evening song,
 Sounding Coulden's woods among;
 Then putting sheep in the pen, let us go,
 My beautiful darling.

Chorus
 Drive the sheep to the hills,
 Drive them where the heather grows,
 Drive them where the stream rolls,
 My beautiful darling.

We'll go down by Clouden side,
 Through the hazels, spreading wide,
 Over the waves that sweetly glide,
 To the moon so clearly.

Chorus

> Drive the sheep to the hills,
> Drive them where the heather grows,
> Drive them where the stream rolls,
> My beautiful darling.

In the distance Clouden's silent towers,
> Where, at moonshine's midnight hours,
> Over the dewy-bending flowers,
> Fairies dance so cheerfully.

Chorus

> Drive the sheep to the hills,
> Drive them where the heather grows,
> Drive them where the stream rolls,
> My beautiful darling.

No ghost or demon shall you fear,
> You are to love and Heaven so dear,
> Nothing of ill may come near you;
> My beautiful darling.

Chorus

>*Drive the sheep to the hills,*
>*Drive them where the heather grows,*
>*Drive them where the stream rolls,*
>*My beautiful darling.*

Fair and lovely as you are,
>*You have stolen my very heart;*
>*I can die, but cannot part,*
>*My beautiful darling.*

Chorus

>*Drive the sheep to the hills,*
>*Drive them where the heather grows,*
>*Drive them where the stream rolls,*
>*My beautiful darling.*

A Little Extra …

In September 1794, Robert sent a copy of this version of the song to George Thompson for inclusion in his book, *"A select collection of original Scottish airs"*.

The original version was sent to James Johnson and was included in his book *"Scots Musical Museum."*

GLOSSARY

One of the biggest barriers to understanding Burns poetry is the old and unusual Scottish dialect he often used. Although, to be fair, he was born over 250 years ago…

This glossary of Scottish words and their modern English translation should help you to break down the language barrier.

A
a' - all
albeit - although
abeigh - at a distance
aboon - above
abide - endure
abread - abrod, in sight
abreed - in breadth
a-bodie - someone
awbodie - everyone
acquent - acquainted
acqueesh - between
a'day - all day long
adle - putrid water
ado - to do

ae - one

aff - off

aff -loof - off hand

afiel - afield

afore - before

aft - often

aften - often

agee - on the side

agley - wrong / askew

ahin - behind

aiblins - perhaps

aik - oak

aiker - acre

ail - ill

ain - own

air - early

airless - money

airn - iron, iron tool

airt - direction

aith - oath

aits - oats

aisle - hot cinder

akwart - awkward

alake - alas

alane - alone

alang - along

alas - sadly

amaist - almost

amang - among

ambrie - cupboard

an - if

an' - and

ance - once

ane - one

ane - own (their)

aneath - beneath

anent - concerning

anes - ones

aneugh - enough

anither - another

ardour - passion

a's - all is

ase - ash

ashet - serving dish

asklent - squint

aspar - spread out

assail - disturb / trouble / attack

aster - stirring

atains - at once

athart - athwart (contradictory)

athole - hawk

at tour - moreover

atweel - of course

aught - possession

aughteen - eighteen

aughtlins - in any way

auld - old

auld reekie - Edinburgh (old smoky)

auld-warld - old-world

aumous - alms, (money or food given to the poor)

aumous-dish - begging bowl

ava - at all

avaunt - Go Away !

awa - away

awald - doubled up

awauk - awake

awe - owe

awfu' - awful

awnie - bearded

awsome - frightful

ayont - beyond

ay - always

B

ba' - ball

babie - baby

babie clouts - baby clothes

backet - bucket

backit - backed

backlins - backwards

bade - asked

baggie - belly

baig'nets - bayonets

baillie - magistrate

bainie - bony

bairn - child / baby

baith - both

bakes- biscuits

ballats - ballads

balloch - mountain pass

bamboozle - confound, trick

ban - curse

ban' - bond

bane - bone

bang - effort

bannet - bonnet

bannock - round flat loaf, cake

barket - barked

barley-bree - whisky

barm - yeast

bartie - the devil

batts - colic

bauchles - old shoes

bauckie-bird - a bat, (flying bat)

baudrons - cat

bauk - rafter

bauld - bold

bawbee - halfpenny

bawk - untiled ridge

baws'nt - white

bawtie - dog

bear / bere - barley

bearded-bere - ripe barley

beas' - vermin

beastie - small animal

beb - drink

bedeen - immediately

beet - fan

beets - boots

befa' - befall

beft - beaten

begrutten - in tears

beik - bask

belang - belong

beld - bald

bellum - assault

bellys - bellows

belyve - quickly / at once

ben - mountain

ben - into, through, within

benison - blessing

bent - field

bere / bear - barley

bestead - provided

bethankit - Give God thanks, grace after a meal

beuk - book

beyont - beyond

bi - by / beside

bi crivens - Christ defend us

bicker (noun) - wooden dish

bicker (verb) - stagger

bickering - argumentative

bide - stay / endure

bield - shelter

bien - prosperous

big - build

biggin - cottage

biggit - built

bill - bull

billie - friend / companion

bing - heap

birk - birch

birken-shaw - small wood

birkie - fellow

birl - carouse

birnie - rough

birr - energy

birses - bristles

bit - place

bizz - bustle

black-bonnet - church elder

blastie - mischievous

blate - bashful

blather - bladder

blathrie - chatter

blatter - rattle

blaud - large quantity

blaw - blow, exaggerate

blawart - bluebell

blest - blessed

blirt - weep / cry

blythe - gentle / kind

blythely - happily / merrily

bocked - vomited

bogle - demon / small monster

bogshaivle - distort

bonie - beautiful

bony - beautiful

boreas - the north wind

bosom - chest / breasts

bow-hough'd - bandy-legged

brachens - ferns

brae - slope, hillside

braid - broad

braid-claith - broad cloth

braird - first sprouting of corn / barley – etc

braik - harrow

braindg't - reeled

brainge - barge

brak - break

brander - gridiron (a frame of parallel bars)

brands - calf muscles

brang - bought

brankan - prancing

branks - halter (a strap or rope around the head of an animal)

brankie - gaudy / smart

brash - illness

brats - scraps

brattle - scamper / run

brattle - chatter / talk

braw - beautiful / handsome

brawlie - heartily

braxie - dead sheep

breastie - breast

breastit - sprang / jumped

brechame - halter

breckan - fern

bree - juice, (whisky)

breeks - britches / trousers

brent - smooth, high

brent -new- brand-new

brig - bridge

briss - press

brither - brother

brock - badger

brogue - trick / fool

broo - broth

brose - oatmeal dish

browden - fond / like

brownie - spirit

browst - ale / beer

brugh - burgh

brulzie - brawl / fight

brunstane - brimstone

brunt - burned

brust - burst

buff - thump

bught - pen

bughtin-time - milking-time

buirdly - stoutly

buller - bubble

bumbazed - confused

bum - clock- beetle

bummin - humming

bummle - useless person

bung - fuddled / confused

bunker - window-seat

burdie - bird / girl

bure - bore

burn - stream / brook

burnewin - blacksmith

burnie - small stream / small burn (stream)

burr-thrissle - thistle

busk - dress

buskie - bushy

buskit - dressed

buss - bush

bussle - bustle

but an' ben - kitchen & parlour

butching - butchering

byke - hive / nest

C

ca' - call

cadger - hawker

caddie - carrier / bearer

caff - chaff

cairn - pile of stones

cairts - playing cards

calf-ward - calf-pen, (enclosure)

callant - a youth (boy)

caller - bracing / cold

callet - girlfriend

cangle - wrangle

cankert - ill tempered

canna - cannot

cannie - cautious / go easy

cannie - gentle

cantie - jolly / happy

cantraip - magic spell

cape-stane - coping stone

careerin' - rushing

care na - care not

carfuffle - disorder / argument

cark - anxious

carle - old man

carline - old woman

cartes - playing cards

castock - cabbage stem

caudron - cauldron

cauf - calf

cauk - chalk

cauld - cold

cavie - coop (hen)

causey - causeway / street

ceilidh - dance / gathering

chafts - chops

chancy - fortune

change-house - ale-house / pub

chantan - chanting

chanters - bagpipes

chap (noun) - liquid measure

chap (verb) - rap / knock

chapman - pedlar

chaup - stroke

cheek-for-chow – cheek-by-jowl

chiel - fellow / man

chimla - fireplace

chimla-lug - fireside

chirm - sing

chittering - shivering

chuck - dear

chuffie - fat-faced

cit - citizen

clachan - village (small)

claes - clothes

claith - cloth

clank (ie) - knock

clarty / clartie - dirty

clash - chatter

clashmaclavers - gossip

claught - seized

claut - clean

claver - clover

clavers - tales / stories

cleed - clothe

cleek - clutch

cleekit - linked arms

cleuch - ravine

clink - coin / money

clinkin - jerking

clinkumbell - bell-ringer

clinty - stony

clips - shears

clash-ma-claver – nonsense

cloot - hoof

clout - patch

cluds - clouds

coft - bought

cog - wooden cup

commaun - command

coman - coming

comely - pleasing

cood - cud

coof - idiot / fool

cookit - hid

coor - cover

cooser - stallion

coost - cast

corbie - crow

core - crowd

corn't - fed with oats

cotter - cottage-dweller (someone who lives in a cottage)

coulter - plough blade

couthie - aggreeable / pleasant

covert - hiding place / conceal

cowe - scare / frighten

cowpit - stumbled

cow'rin - cowering

cowslip - yellow flowers

cozie - comfortable / warm

crabbit - miserable / negative

crack - conversation

craft - croft

craig - rock

craigie - throat

crambo-jingle - rhymes

cranks - creaking

cranreuch - hoar-frost / frost

crap - crop

craw - crow

creel - basket / confusion

creeshie - greasy

cronie - friend

croon - hum

crouchie - hunchbacked

crouse - merry

crowdie - porridge

crowl - crawl

crummie - cow

crummock - crooked staff

crump - crisp

cry - tell

culzie - flatter

cuif - idiot / fool

cun - earn

curch - kerchief

curmurring - commotion

curn - parcel

curple - buttocks

cutled - courted

cutty - short

D

dab - peck / pierce

daez't - bewildered

daffin - merriment

dail - plank

daidlin - waddling

daimen-icker - occasional ear of corn

dam - pent up water

dams - game of draughts

damn'd haet - damn all

dang - pushed / knocked

darg - work

darger - casual laborer

darklin - dark

daud - pelt

daunder - stroll / walk

daunton - subdue

daur - dare

daurt - dared

daut - fondle / pet

daver - wander aimlessly

dawd - lump

dawt - caress

dawin - dawning

dearthfu' - expensive

deave - deafen

defac'd - defaced

Deil - Devil

deleerit - delirious

delvin - digging

deray - disorder

dern - hidden

descrive - describe

deuk - duck

deval - descend

diddle - move quickly

differ - quarrel / dispute

dight - wipe / clean

dimpling - undulating

dink - trim

dinmont - two year old sheep

dinna - don't

dint - affection

dirk - short dagger

dizzen - dozen

docht - dared

dochter - daughter

doit - small copper coin

doited - muddled

donsie - self important

doo - dove

dool - sorrow

douce - prudent / grave

douk - duck

doup - backside

dou / doo - dove

douk - dip / bathe

dour - sullen / unhappy

dow - can

dowff - dismal

downa - cannot

doxy - lover / suitor

doylt - stupid

doytin - doddering

draigl't - draggled / unkempt

drants - long prayers

drap - drop

draunting - drawling

dree - suffer

dreeping - dripping

dreigh - tedious

drest - dressed

driddle - saunter / walk slow

drod - prick

droddum - backside / bum
droukit - drenched / soaked
drouth - thirst
drucken - drunken
drum - hillock / ridge
drumlie - muddy
drummock - oatmeal & water
drunt - bad mood
dub - puddle
duddies - ragged old clothes
dunt - hit / strike a blow
durk - dirk / short dagger
dusht - pushed / thrown
dwaum - swoon / feint
dyke - wall / dry stone wall
dynie - tremble
dyvor - Bankrupt

E

ear' - early
eard - earth
eastlin - eastern
e'ebrie - eyebrow
e'e - eye
een - eyes
e'en - even
e'enin - evening

eenou - immediately

eerie - strange / frightening

efface - erase

eggle - urge on

eke - also

eild - old age

elbuck - elbow

eldritch - unearthly

elekit - elected

eller - church elder

embower - surround / shelter

en' - end

eneugh - enough

enow - enough

erselins - backwards

esthler - carved stone

etter - fester

ettercap - spider

ettle - aim

even'd - compare

evermair - evermore

evite - shun

expeckit - expected

eydent - diligent

F

fa' - fall / to get / lot

fab - trick

faddom - fathom

fae - from / foe / enemy

faem - foam

faiket - let off / excused

fail - turf

fain - affectionate / fond

fair-fa' - welcome / good luck

fairin - present / reward

fairly - certainly

fairmers - farmers

fait - neat

faize - annoy / upset

fan - found

fand - found (past tense)

fank - sheep pen / rope coil

fankle - tangle

fantoush - flashy

farden - farthing

farl - scone / small oatcake

fash - trouble / irritate

fasht - troubled / bothered

Fasten-ee'ne - Shrove Tuesday

fat - what

fatt'rills - ribbons

fauld - fold

faun - fallen

faur - far

faur back - long ago

fause - false

faut - fault

fawsont - seemly

feal - field

fear't - frightened

fecht - fight

feck - majority / the bulk

fecket - waistcoat

feckless - weak

feerie - sturdy

feide - fued

feil - many

feirrie - lusty

fell - deadly

felly - relentless

fent - garment opening

ferlie - wonder / marvel

fernyer - last year

fetter - bind / chain

fettle - condition

fey - fated

fickle - changeable

fidgin-fain - restless

fiel - comfortable

fient - devilish

fier - well / friend

filial - dutiful

findy - substantial

fissle - tingle

fit - foot

flacht - handful

flait / flate - scolded

flawgaires - whimsies

fleesh - fleece

fleg - frighten

flesher - butcher

fletherin - flattering

fley'd - frightened

flichtering - fluttering

flinders - shreds

flinty - hard

fliskit - fretted

flit - move

fluther - hurry

flyte - scold

fodgel - plump

foggage - a second growth of grass

fon - fond

Foorsday - Thursday

for a' that - not withstanding

foraye - forever

Forfairn - worn out

forfouchen - exhausted

forgather - meet

forker - earwig

forleet - forsake

fou - drunk / full

foughten - troubled

fouth - plenty

frae - from

frammle - gobble

frist - trust

fu' - drunk / full

fud - backside (short tail)

fushion - vigour / spirit

fusionless - spiritless / weak

fustit - decayed

fyke - fidget

fyled - soiled / fouled

G

gab - talk / mouth

gae - go

gadsman - ploughboy

gallants - splendid men

gan - begun

gane - gone

gang - go

gangrel - vagrant

gar - make

gars - makes

gash - respectable

gat - got

gate - road

gath'rin - gathering

gaud - went

gauger - exciseman

gaun - going

gawky - akward

gawsie - jolly / buxom

gear - belongings

gentie - graceful

genty - trim / elegent

get - child / offspring

ghaist - ghost

gie - give

gif - if

gilpey - young woman

gin - against

girn - grin

girnal - meal chest

grin - snarl

glaikit - foolish

glaum'd - snatched

glen - valley

gloaming - twilight

glunch - frown

gowan - daisy

gowd - gold

gowden - golden

gowdie - head

gowdspink - goldfinch

gracefu' - graceful

graff - grave

graith - harness

grat - wept / cried

gree - prize

greet - weep

grippit - mean

grozet - gooseberry

gropsy - glutton

guddle - mess / mangle

gude - god

guid - good

guidman - master of the house

guid-willie waught – cup of kindness / goodwill drink

gully - large knife

gumlie - muddy

gumption - commonsense

gurlie - rough

gut-scraper - fiddler

gyte - insane / mad

H

ha' - Hall

habber - stutter

haddie - Haddock (fish)

haddin - piossesion

hadna - had not

hae - have

haerst - harvest

haffet - lock of hair

hafflins - halfway

hag - moss

hain - spare

hald - property / hold

hale - fit / hearty

hallow mass - all Saints day

hame - home

han - hand

hand-wal'd - hand picked

hankers - desires

hap - wrap

haply - perhaps / by any chance

harigals - entrails

harkit - listened

hash - oaf / idiot

haster - perplex

haud - hold

hauffet - temple

haugh - low lying meadow by a river

haughs - hollows

haurl - drag

havins - manners

hear'st - do you hear

hee - call

heeze - raise

hen-shin'd - bow-legged

here awa - here about / near

heugh - crag

hinderlets - hind parts

hindmost - last

hing - hang

hinny - honey

hirplin - limping

hizzie - hussy / slag

hoar - frost

hoary - greyish white / silvery

hoast - cough

hool - the husk

hornie - devil

houlet - owl

housal - household

hov'd - swollen

howdie - midwife

howe - hollow / glen

howk - dig

hunkers - haunches
hurdies - buttocks
hure - whore
hurl - throw / crash

I

Icker - ear of corn
ier-oe - great grandchild
ilk - each
ilka - every
ill-deedy - mischievous
ill-willy - ill-natured
ingle - fireplace
ingle-gleede - blazing fireside
ingle-lowe - fire light
intermix'd - intermixed
inviolate's - untouched
ither - other
izles - embers

J

Jad - old horse
jag - pin prick
jauk - daily
jaup - splash
jaw - insolent talk

jawpish - tricky
jimplly - neatly
jinglan - jingling
jink - dodge
jo - sweetheart
jockey-coat - overcoat
jocteleg - clasp knife
jouk - dodge
jow - swing
jumpit - jumped

K

kae - jackdaw (bird)
kail - cabbage
kail-whittle - cabbage knife
kail-yard - cabbage patch
kain - rents in kind
kame - comb
katy-handit - left handed
kebars - rafters
kebbuck - cheese
keek - peep / look
keekin' glass - mirror
keel - chalk
Keen - sharp / eager
keepit - kept
kelpies - water spirits

ken - know

ken't - knew

kenspeckle - easily recognized

ket - fleece

kiaugh - anxiety / worry

kin - relatives / family members

kinch - noose

kindred - family

kintra - country

kirk - church

kirn - harvest supper

kirsen - chisten

kiss caups - pledge friendship

kist - chest

kith - acquaintance / friend

kittle (adj) - difficult

Kittle (noun) - tickle

knaggie - nobly

knap - smart blow

knapper - head

knoited - knocked

knowe - hillock

knurl - dwarf

kye - cow

kyte - belly

L

Lac'd - corseted

lade - load

lady-landers - ladybird

laggen - bottom of a dish

laigh - low

laiglen - milking pail / bucket

lairing - sinking

laith - loath / hate

lallan - lowland

lammas - August 1st / harvest

lammie - lamb

landlowper - vagabond / tramp

lane - lone

lang - long

lang syne - long ago

langsum - tedious / boring

lantron - lantern / light

laughan - laughing

laun - land

lave - remainder / rest of

laverock - skylark (bird)

law - hill

lawin - bill

lea' - leave

leal - loyal

lear - learning

lee-lang - live long

leesome - pleasant

leeve - live

leeze - bless

leister- spear

len' - lend

leugh - laugh

leuk - look

libbet - gelded / castrated

lightsome - carefree

limmer - mistress

linket - skipped

linn - waterfall

lint - flax / linseed plant

lippen - trust

loan - lane

loof - palm

loon / loun - lad /roguish boy

loot - allow

loup / lowp - leap / jump

lov'd - loved

lov'st - loves

lowe - flame

lowse - loose

luckie - old woman

luesom - lovely

lug - ear

lugget - having ears

luggie - two handled cup

lum - chimney

luntin - smoking

lume - loom

lure - rather

lurve - love

lyart - grey / withered / old

lye - lie

M

mae - more

Mahoun - Devil

maik - equal

mair - more

maist - most

maister - master

mak - make

mak'sna - matters not

mantie - gown

mang - among

manna - food from God

manteel - mantle

mantling - foaming

maskin pat - tea pot

maught - might

maukin - hare

maun - must

maunna - must not

maut - malt

mavis - thrush / bird

mere / meare - mare / female horse

meikle - large

mein - look / demeanour

men' - mend

mense - sense / tact

menseless - senseless

menzie - follower

merk - old Scottish coin

mess John - church minister

middin - dunghill / scrapheap

middlins - moderately

milkin' shiel - milking parlour

mim - meek

mim mou'd - gently spoken

min' - remember

mind - bear in mind

mindna - forget

Minnie - mother

mirk - gloom

misca' - abuse

mishanter - mishap / accident

mislear'd - unmannerly / rude

mislippen - disappoint

mismarrow - mismatch

mistaen - mistaken

mith - might

mither - mother

moch - moist

monie - many

mony - many

moolin - crumb

mools - dust

moop - nibble

moosty - mouldy

mottle - dusty

mou' - mouth

moubit - mouthful

moudiwort - mole

muckle - great

muir - moor

mumpit - stupid

musing - thinking

muslin - kail- thin broth (soup)

mutchkin - English pint

mysel - myself

N

na' - not

nack - trick

nae - no

naebody - nobody

naething - nothing

naig - pony

naither - neither

nane - none

nappy - ale / beer

nar - near

nay - no / or rather

neebor - neighbor

needfu' - needful

needna - need not

negleck - neglect

neist - next

neth - below

neuk - corner

newlins - very lately

nicht - night

nick - small cut

nicket - cheated

niest - next

nieve - fist

niffer - exchange

nit - nut

nocht - nought

noddle - brain

norlan - northland

notour - notorious

nourice - nurse

nowte - cattle

nowther - neither

O

o'boot - gratis / free

ocht - aught

ochtlins - in the least

o'erhung - overhung

o'erlay - smock /dress

o'erword - chorus

onie - any

or - before

orra - extra

o't - of it

oughtlins - in the same degree

ouk - week

ourie - shivery

oursels - ourselves

out - owre- above

owre - over

owsen - oxen

owther - either

owthor - author

oxter - armpit

P

pack - intimate

paction - agreement

paidle (noun) - puddle

paidle (verb) - dawdle

painch - paunch / large belly paitrick- partridge (bird)

pang - cram

parishen - parish

parritch - porridge

pash - head

pat - pot

pattle - plough staff / stick

paughty - proud

pawkie - cunning

pechan - stomach

pechin - out of breath

peet mow - peat stack

peinge - whine

peltry - trash

penny fee - wages

penny wheep - small beer

pensfu' - conceited

philibeg - kilt

phoebus - Apollo / the sun

phraise - flatter

pickle - small quantity

pimpin - low / mean

pine - pain

pinion - cog / part of a birds wing

pint stowp - pint measure

pit - put

plack - pennies

plackless - penniless

pleugh / plew - plough

plouk - pimple / spot

plover - short billed wading bird

poacher court - Kirk Session

pock - pocket

poind - seized

pooch - pouch

pook - pluck

poortith - poverty

pou - pull

pouk - poke / jab

poupit - church pulpit

pouse - push

poussie - hare / cat

pouther - powder

pow - head

pownie - pony

pree'd - tasted

preen - pin

presses - cupboards

preeve - prove

prent - print

prief - proof

prigging - haggling

prostration - subservience

pu' - pull

pultrous - lecherous

pund - pound

pursie - small purse

pussie - hare

pyke - pick

pyle - grain

pystle - epistle

Q

quaite - quiet

quat - quit / give up

quauk - quake / shake

quey - cow

quine - young woman

quer - choir

quo - quoth / humorous

R

rade - rode

raff - plenty

raffan - hearty

ragweed - ragwort

raible - nonsense

rair - roar

ramfeezl'd - exhausted

ramgunshoch - rugged

rampin' - ragging / angry

ram stam - headlong

randie - riotous

rankling - festering

rape- rope

raploch - home-spun

rarely - quickly

rash - rush

rattle - strike / hit

ratton - rat

raucle - fearless

raught - reached

raw - row

rax - stretch

ream - froth

reave - rob / steal

red / rede - advise

reek - smoke / smell

remead - remedy

reuth - pity

richt - right

rief - thieve

rig - ridge

rigs - ridges

riggin - roof

rin - run

ringle-ey'd - white-eyed

ripp - handful of corn

riskit - cracked

rither - rudder

rive - split

roon - round

roose - reputation

roosty - rusty

roving - walking / wandering

rowth - plenty

rowtin - lowing

rozet - rosin

rugh - rough

rullions - coarse shoes

rummle - stir about

rummlegumption - common sense

run - downright

rung - cudgel / weapon

runkle - wrinkle

ruth - sorrow

ryke - reach

S

sab - sob /cry loudly

sae - so

saebins - since it is so

saft - soft

saikless - innocent

sair (verb) - serve

sair (adj) - sore / hard

sairie - sorrowful

sall - shall

sark - shirt

saul - soul

saumont - salmon (fish)

saunt - saint

saut - salt

saw - sow / plant seeds

sax - six

scail - spill

scaith - injury

scantlins - scarcely

scar - scare

sconner - disgust / annoy

scotia - Scotland

scraichin - screaming

scrievin - moving along

scrimpt - short / cut back

sculduggery - fornication

see'd - saw

seelfu - pleasant

seenle - seldom

see'st - do you see

session - court

set - start

shachl't - distorted

shanks - legs

shanna - shall not

shaul - shallow

shavie - trick / prank

shaw - small group of trees

shaw (noun) - woodland

shaw (verb) - show

shawpit - shelled

shaws - stalks

sheugh - ditch

sheuk - shook

shiel - shed

shool - shovel

shoon - shoes

shor'd - threaten

shot - sort

shouldna - should not

shouther - sholder

sic / sik - such

sicker - steady

sidelins - sideways

siller - silver

simmer - summer

sin - since

sirple - sip

skaith- damage / mark

skeigh - skittish / nervous

skellum - rogue

skelpin - rushing

skelvy - layered

skilly - skillful

skinking - watery

skinklin - small

skirl - shriek

sklent - side-look

skrimmish - skirmish / fight

skurrivaig - vagabond / tramp

skyre - shine

skyte - lash

slade - slid

slae - sloe

slaik - lick

slap - gap

slaw - slow

slee - sly

sleekit - sneaky/ smooth / cunning

sloken - slake / quench thirst

sma' - small

smack - kiss

smawly - small

smeddum - powder / malt dust

smeek - smoke

smiddie / smiddy - blacksmith

smirtle - shy smile

smoor - smother

smurr - drizzle

smytrie - group / collection

snakin - sneering

snash - abuse

snaw - snow

sned - cut off

snell - bitter / biting / sharp

sneshin - snuff

snick - latch

snirtle - snigger

snool - snub

snowkit - snuffed

sodger - soldier

sole - sill

sonnet - song

sonsie - pleasant

soom - swim

soor - sour

souk - suck

souple - supple

souter - cobbler / shoe maker

sowp - spoonful

sowther - solder

spae - foretell

spair - spare

spak - spoke

sparely - sparsely

spean - wean / get used to

speat - spate

speel - climb

speet - skewer

speir - ask

spelder - tear apart

spence - parlour

spleuchan - tobacco pouch

splore - frolic / carousal

sprattle - scramble

spreckle - speckled

spirritie - full of spirits

sprush - dressed up

spunk - spirit

spunkie - will o' the wisp

squattle - squat

stab - stake (wooden)

Stacher - stagger

stan' - stand

stane - stone

stang - sting

stank - pool

stap - stop

stapple - stopper

stark - strong

staumrel - silly

staw - sicken

stechin - cramming

steek - stitch

steer - stir

steeve - compact

stell - still

stent - duty

steyest - steepest

stibble - stubble

stickit - stuck

stimpart - quarter measure

stirk - young cow

stoiter - stumble

stotter - stagger

stoun / stown - stolen

stounds - aches

stoure - dust / battle

stown - stolen

stowp - cup

strae - straw

stak - stuck

staike - stroke

stramash - argument / fight

strang - strong

straught - straight

stravaugin - roaming

streekit - stretched

streen - last night

striddle - straddle

studdie - anvil

stumle - stumble

stump - stop / halt

stumpie - stout

sturt - fret / worry

sucker - sugar

sugh - sigh

sumph - blockhead / idiot

sune - soon

suthron - southern

swall'd - swelled

swain - suitor / lover

swally - swallow / drink

swankie - fine fellow

swarf - to swoon

swat - sweat

swatch - sample / little bit

swats - light beer

swee - over

sweer - lazy

swith - get away

swither - hesitate

swoor - swore

syne - since / then

T

tack - lease

tackets - shoe-nails

tae - toe

taen - taken

taigle - hinder

taikle - tackle

tairge - target

taisle - tassel

tak - take

tald - told

tangs - tongs

tap - top

tapetless - thoughtless

tapsalteerie - topsy-turvy

tassie - cup

tauk - talk

tauld - told

teat - small quantity

ted - spread

teen - sorrow / grief

teen - anger

tensum - ten together

tent (noun) - caution

tent (verb) - tend

tentie - careful

tentless - without a care

teugh - tough

teuk - took

thack - thatch

thae - those

thairm - intestines

thankit - thanked

thegither - together

thereanet - about that

thick - inmate

thieveless - forbidding

thiggin - begging

thir - these

thirl - thrill

tho' - although

thocht - thought

thole - endure / suffer

thon - you

thou'se - thou shalt

thowe - thaw

thrang (noun) - a crowd

thrang (verb) - busy

thrapple - throat

thrave - 24 sheaves of corn

thraw - twist

threed - thread

threep - maintain

threesum - three together

threteen - thirteen

thretty - thirsty

thrist - thirst

thrissle - thistle

throu'ther - confused

thumpit - thumped

thurst - thrust

thysel - thyself / yourself

timmer - timber

timmer-tuned - unmusical

tim'rous - fearful

tip / toop - ram (tup) / a sheep

tipper - taiper- teeter

tine - lose

tinkler - tinker / tramp

tint - lost

tippence - two pence

tippenny - two-penny beer

tir - tap

'tis - it is

tither - other

tittle - whisper

tocher - marriage bonds

tod - fox

Tod Lowrie - fox

too fa' - lean-to

toom - empty

tother - other

toun - farmland

towsie/tousie - shaggy

tow - rope

towsing - handling

towmound - twelve-month

toy - cap

tozie - tipsy

traiket - disordered

trashtrie - rubbish

trepan - ensnare

trig - neat

trowth - trust

tryste - appointment

try't - tried

tuffle - ruffle

tulzie - quarrel

tummle - tumble

tummler - cup / glass

tunefu' - tuneful

ture - tore

turkasses - pincers

turn - task

turrs - turfs

twa / tway - two

'twad - would have

twahaund - between two

twal - twelve

twasum - two together

tween - between

tweesh - betwixt / between

twin - sepatate from

twine - twist

tyesday - Tuesday

tyke - dog

tyken - bed linen

tylie - slice of beef

tyest - entice

U

ulzie - oil

unchancy - dangerous

unco - strange / very

undeemous - inconceivable

undocht - silly

uneith - difficult

unfauld - unfold

unfeiry - inactive

unkend - unknown

unkin - unkind

unloosome - unlovely / ugly

unsicker - uncertain

unsneck - unlock

unweeting - unwittingly

uphaud - uphold

upo' - upon

upsides - equal to

upstan't - stood

uptack - understanding

usquebah - whisky

V

van - group

vauntie - proud

vera / verra - very

verdant - green / lush

vernal - springtime

vernal - youthful

vie - compete

virl - ring

vittles - food

vively - clearly

vogie - conceited

vowt - vault / jump

W

wa' - wall

wab - web

wabster - weaver

wad - wager

wad - would

waddin' - wedding

wadna - would not

wae - woe /sorrow

weaness - sadness

waesucks - alas

wair'd - spent

wale - choice

walie - large

wame - belly

wan - won / one

wanchancie - dangerous

wanrestfu' - restless

wanruly - unruly

wanton - promiscuous / frolic deliberate

wanwordy - unworthy

wap - wrap

wappon - weapon

war - were

ware - worn

wark - work

warl' / warld - world

war's gear - worldly possesions

warlock-breef - magic spell

warl'y - worldly

warna - were not

warran - warrant

warse - worse

warsle - wrestle

wart - were it

wast - west

wat - wet

water-fit - mouth of the river

waud - wade

waugh - damp

waught - large dink

wauk - wake

waukrife - sleepless

waukit - calloused

waur - worse

wawlie - handsome

wean - child

weary fa' - plague upon

weason - gullet

wecht - weight

wee - small

weed - clothes

weel - well

weel-hain'd - well-saved

weet - wet

westlin - westerly

wha - who

whae - who

whaizle - wheeze

whalpit - whelped / birthed

whang - slice

whan - when

whar - where

whase - whose

whaup - curlew / bird

whid - fib / move quickly

whigmaleeries - whimsical

whiles - sometimes / at times

whilk - which

whirligigums - useless things

whisht - silence

whitter - measure of liquor

whommilt - turned upside down

whun - basalt / volcanic rock

whunner - rattle

whup - whip

whyles - sometimes

wi' - with

wifie - wife

willyart - awkward

wimple (verb) - wind

wimplin - winding

winch - wench

winna - will not

winnins - earnings / winnings

winnock-bunker – window seat

win's - winds

wise-like - respectable

wiss - wish

written - knowledge

wonner - wonder

woo' - wool

woodie - gallows

wook - weak

wordy - worthy

wrack - vex / annoy

wraith - spirit

wrang - wrong

wran - wren / song bird

wright - carpenter

writer - lawyer

wud - wild

wuddie - rope

wull - will

wure - wore

wursum - putrid

wurtle - writhe / squirm

wyliecoat - flannel vest

wyle - entice / attract

wyss - wise

wyte - blame

Y

Yad - old mare

yaird - yard

yarrow - white flower

yauld - vigorous

yaumer - murmur

ye - you

ye'd - you would

ye'll - you will

yell - barren / empty

yellockin - squalling

yer - your

yersel - yourself

ye'se - ye shall / you shall

yestereen - last evening / night

yett - gate

yill - ale

yince - once

yird - earth

yirdit - buried

yokin - set to

yon - that

yonner - yonder

'yont - beyond

younker - youth

yowe - ewe / a sheep

yowie - lamb / young sheep

ABOUT THE AUTHOR

Alastair Turnbull

Alastair Turnbull is a Scotsman and author of Non Fiction books. These books are usually on the subjects of **Scotland**, **Drinking** and **Robert Burns**. These also happen to be three of Alastair's greatest passions in life - after his **wife** and two **daughters**.

Alastair lives in Scotland and has been self-employed for over 15 years in the conference, events and exhibition industry. Working as an Audio-Visual technician he has travelled the globe working with a large variety of companies from pharmaceuticals to wind energy specialists, solicitors to potato farmers. If you have no idea what that actually means, just think of him as a corporate "roadie". For example, the picture above was taken whilst working as a camera-man at an event held at "The Kelpies", near Falkirk, Scotland.

Alastair started his writing career with the web site:

This site, which is still very much alive and well, was born after working at endless road shows and events with Scottish drinks producers. There was only so much information he could take in before it started to pour out onto web pages and then onto ebooks and magazines. After writing about the great drinks Scotland has to offer, he then started writing about his other two passions: Scotland and Robert Burns.

In his free time Alastair likes to spend time with his family and indulge his three passions. This usually involves him dragging them around yet another Distillery / Brewery / Cider Mill in Scotland, whilst telling them how this relates to Robert Burns work as an excise man.

His family doesn't always enjoy spending time with him.

Christine & Alastair Turnbull

A Little Extra...

Alastair's wife's maiden name is Christine Burns.
Christine's fathers name was **Robert Burns**. He was a
farmer from Renfrewshire, (next to Ayrshire).

For more information please contact me.

www.TheDrinkingMansGuideToScotland.com

Robert Burns - Women:
This is the first book in the series "**Enjoying Robert Burns**".
This highlights twelve works by Robert Burns, which were inspired by women in his life. In the book we look at the women behind the poems, their relationship with Burns and what happened to them. It also includes a modern English translation of each poem and an extensive glossary.

There are more books planned in the series "**Enjoying Robert Burns** ". They are:

Robert Burns - Food & Drink
Robert Burns - Life
Robert Burns - Death
Robert Burns - Scotland

Other Books by Alastair Turnbull:

Toasts & Toasting – A Simple Guide to Toasts, Blessings & Graces

This book is a guide to making a toast, whether it be at a wedding, birthday, graduation, funeral, etc. It also looks at Blessings, Graces, toasting traditions and toasting folklore.

Alastair Turnbull also writes for the web site:
TheDrinkingMansGuideToScotland.com

Printed in Great Britain
by Amazon